My Writer's Journal

By _____

All About Me

By _____

WRITER'S ACTIVITY BOOK

WORLD
OF
LANGUAGE

SILVER BURDETT & GINN

MORRISTOWN, NJ • NEEDHAM, MA
Atlanta, GA • Cincinnati, OH • Dallas, TX • Menlo Park, CA • Deerfield, IL

CONTENTS

——— INTRODUCTORY UNIT ———

——— UNIT 1 ———

——— UNIT 2 ———

——— UNIT 3 ———

——— UNIT 4 ———

——— UNIT 5 ———

——— UNIT 6 ———

UNIT 7

UNIT 8

BOOK COVERS

ALL ABOUT ME

My Picture

My name is _____ .

The Seasons

This is what I like to do.

ALL ABOUT ME

My School

The name of my school is _____

Toys and Games

Here are three toys I like.

I can tell about a game I like to play.

_____

_____

_____

_____

_____

_____

_____

_____

My Favorites

_____

- -

My favorite color is _____.

_____

- -

My favorite book is _____.

_____

- -

My favorite sport is _____.

_____

- -

My favorite food is _____.

These are my favorites, too.

_____   _____

- - - - - - - - - - - -   - - - - - - - - - - - -

_____   _____

Growing Up

This is what I want to do when I grow up.

I want to be
_____
- -
_____.

A journal is a book you can write in.

You can write about your wishes
or your favorite lunch-time dishes.

You can write about playtime or bedtime.
You can write a story or a funny rhyme.
You can write anything you want.

You can draw pictures in your journal.
You can paste pictures in it, too!

A journal is a special book.
It is yours!

◆ A WRITER'S JOURNAL ◆

You can make a journal.

You will need:

This is what to do:

1. Pull out the covers.

2. Put paper between them.

3. Line up the holes.

4. Tie the paper inside.

5. Write your name.

6. Color the cover.

Now you are ready to write!

You can make a writing folder, too. You will save pages from this book in it. When you see this ◆SAVE◆, remember to save the page in your Writing Folder.

INTEREST INVENTORY

What will you write about?
Here are some ideas.
Circle the pictures that show what
you like best.

1. I like

2. I like

3. I like

4. I like

5. I like

6. I like

7. I like

8. I like books about

9. I also like

You see many kinds of writing every day.
Here are some of them.
Talk about each one.
Which one would you like to try?

Mom,
Dad called. He
will be home at
7:00 P.M.

Lost cat
yellow and black
If found, please
call 555-8702.

Dear Uncle Dave,
I hope you get better
soon.

Love,
Sally

Keep Out!

Please come to my party.
Saturday, November 13.
2:00-4:00 P.M.
Sally Leland
786 Elm Street

Class 1A
9:00   Reading
10:00   Math
11:00   Gym
12:00   Lunch

Pancakes
1 cup flour
1 cup milk
1 egg
1 tablespoon oil
Mix and cook on
hot griddle.

I saw a lion at the zoo.

Here are some other writing forms.

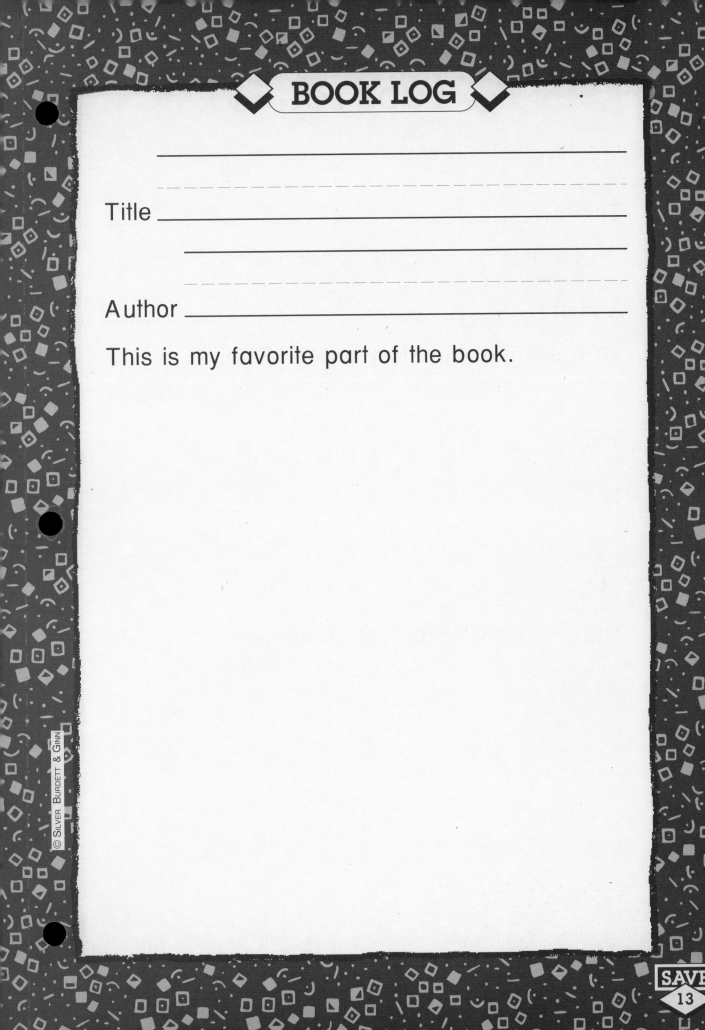

◆ BOOK LOG ◆

Title _____

Author _____

This is my favorite part of the book.

Title _____

Author _____

This is where the story takes place.

These are the important characters.

Name _____

Creating

What do you see?
Finish the sentence.
You may use a rhyming word.
You will find some in the poems you just listened to.

Look what I see.

_____

_____

I see a _____ .

Now draw your own cloud picture.
Use the back of this sheet.

Checking My Work ✔
Did I use
◇ sentences ☐
◇ capitals ☐
◇ ⋅ or ? ☐

Look what I see.

_____

- -

I see a _____ .

© SILVER BURDETT & GINN

Speaking in Complete Sentences

Find each sentence.
Write it correctly.
Remember that a sentence tells a complete story.

1. I bear
saw
I saw a bear.

_____

- - - - - - - - - - - -

_____

2. A man fed the lions.
fed the lions.
A man

_____

- - - - - - - - - - - -

_____

3. rode on
I rode on the sky ride.
the sky ride.

_____

- - - - - - - - - - - -

_____

What might you see and do at the zoo?
Draw a picture to complete each sentence.

4. I saw a  .

5. I liked the  .

6. The  swim in the pond.

7. The  are funny.

Telling Sentences

Write telling sentences about the picture.
Remember to begin a sentence with a capital letter.
End a telling sentence with a period.

sunny day

it is a sunny day

Chris has many fish

many fish

Spot no hat

Spot takes a fish

frog jump

a frog jumps on Spot

_____

1._____

_____

2._____

_____

3._____

_____

4._____

Write telling sentences about the picture.
Use the sentence parts that go together.

Spot   makes a fire.
Dad   digs a hole.
Mom   cooks the fish.
Joe   puts up the tent.
Chris   tells a story.

Unit 1, Lesson 8 • Use after page 20.

© SILVER BURDETT & GINN

Asking Sentences

Help Ann write a note to her dad.
Find the asking sentences.
Write each one correctly in the note.
Remember to begin each sentence
with a capital letter.
End each asking sentence with a question mark.

may I go to Liz's house   may I eat dinner there
I hope you will say yes   Liz asked me to visit her
we will play outside   will you come for me at
                              7:00 P.M.

Dear Dad,

_____

- - - - - - - - - - - - - - - - - - -

_____

- - - - - - - - - - - - - - - - - - -

_____

- - - - - - - - - - - - - - - - - - -

_____

- - - - - - - - - - - - - - - - - - -

_____

- - - - - - - - - - - - - - - - - - -

_____

                              Love,

                              Ann

Write a note.

Ask if you can sleep at your friend's house.

Write asking sentences.

Use the words in the box to help.

will	I	sleep	may	house
me	at	park	the	there

_____

- - - - - - - - - - - - - - - -

Dear _____ ,

_____

- -

_____

- -

_____

- -

_____

- -

_____

Love,

_____

- - - - - - - - - - - - - - - -

_____

Unit 1, Lesson 9 • Use after page 22.

Name_____

Classifying

You just listened to a story about forest animals.
Now think about farm animals.
What can each animal do?
On the back of this sheet, draw a farm animal.
Then write what it can do.

Checking My Work ✔

Did I use

◇ sentences ☐

◇ capitals ☐

◇ · or ? ☐

Naming Words

Finish these pages for a class pictionary.
Write the correct naming word.
Remember that a naming word names a person,
place, or thing.

Place   Thing   Person

Bb	Cc	Ff

Make your own pictionary page about a farm.
Draw a person, place, or thing.
Write the first letter of the naming word.
Write the naming word.

Names for People

Pretend that you had a birthday party.
Your family took lots of pictures.
Color the frame around each picture that
shows a person.
Write another word that could name each person.

man mother friend brother woman child grandpa

girl

cake

clown

boy

mom

Here are some more pictures.
Help make a photo album.
Finish the sentence for each picture.
Write a word that names the person or persons.

1. Four _____ come to my party.

2. A _____ does tricks.

3. My _____ carries the cake.

4. Here I am with my _____ .

Names for Places

Find on each postcard the word that
names a place.
Draw a picture of the place.
Remember that words such as **park** and
lake name places.

Dear Lucy,
    I am at Grandpa's
house. It is nice.
I wish you were here.
            Love,
            Meg

Dear Tina,
    Today we walked in
the woods. We saw
a deer! It was pretty.
            Love,
            Meg

Dear Greg,
    I swam in this pond
today. There are fish
in it, too. It is fun!
            Your friend,
            Meg

Make two postcards to send to Meg.
Draw a place where you like to go.
Complete each sentence with the
name of the place.
Remember to sign your name.

Dear Meg,
Today I went to the

_____

- - - - - - - - - - - - - - - -

_____ .

It was fun!
    From, _____

- - - - - - - - - - - - - - -

_____

Dear Meg,
I like to walk around the

_____

- - - - - - - - - - - - - - -

_____ .

See you soon!
    Love, _____

- - - - - - - - - - - - - - -

_____

Unit 2, Lesson 9 • Use after page 46.

Names for Things

Help Hal pack his suitcase.
Write the words that name the things
Hal should pack.
Remember that words such as **hat**
and **car** name things.

shirt

pants

parrot

shoes

socks

pajamas

comb

cat

grandma

1._____

2._____

3._____

4._____

5._____

6._____

Pretend you are going on a trip.
Pack a suitcase.
Draw things that you will need.
Label the things you draw.

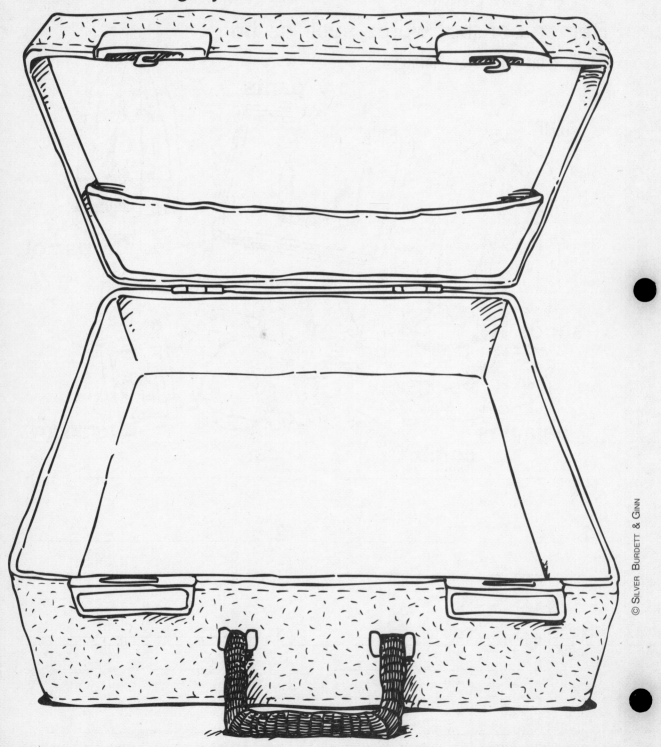

© Silver Burdett & Ginn

Unit 2, Lesson 10 • Use after page 47.

Compounds

Look at the picture.
Write the compound.
Remember that a compound is
a word made from two words.

 +

1. house   boat
_____
- - - - - - - - - - - - - - - -
_____

 +

2. house   fly
_____
- - - - - - - - - - - - - - - -
_____

 +

3. light   house
_____
- - - - - - - - - - - - - - - -
_____

 +

4. dog   house
_____
- - - - - - - - - - - - - - - -
_____

 +

5. bird   house
_____
- - - - - - - - - - - - - - - -
_____

Make your own puzzles.
Find compounds that you can
make from words in the box.
Draw a picture for each word.
Write the compound.

foot	door	tooth	cow	pig	rain
boy	ball	brush	tail	bell	bow

6.
☐ + ☐
= _____

7.
☐ + ☐
= _____

8.
☐ + ☐
= _____

Unit 2, Lesson 11 • Use after page 48.

One or More Than One

Find the T-shirts that name one thing.

Color them 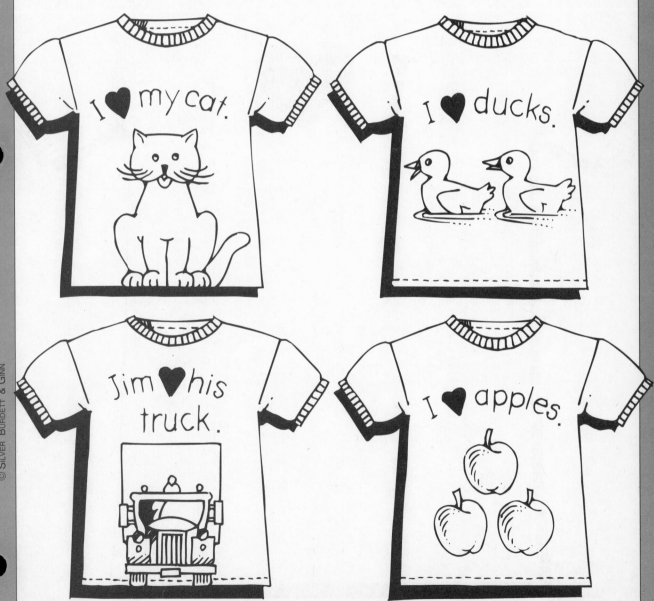 Red .

Find the T-shirts that name more than one thing.

Color them Blue .

Remember that many words add **s** to

mean more than one.

I ♥ my cat.

I ♥ ducks.

Jim ♥ his truck.

I ♥ apples.

Think about something that you like very much.
Make a T-shirt.
Write a word for more than one on your T-shirt.
Draw a picture, too.

I ♥

Unit 2, Lesson 12 • Use after page 50.

Name

Narrating

You just read about a little bear.
Look at the bear in this picture.
What do you think will happen next?
On the back of this sheet, draw a picture about it.
Finish the sentence that tells what the bear does.

© SILVER BURDETT & GINN

Checking My Work ✔

Did I use

◇ sentences ☐

◇ capitals ☐

◇ · or ? ☐

The bear _____

_____

_____ .

Name _____

Writing Sentences for a Picture Story

Read each question. Check ☑ if you can answer yes.

- ☐ Did I write about my favorite part of the story?
- ☐ Do I need to add any words?
- ☐ Do I want to change any words?
- ☐ Did I make a neat copy of my writing?
- ☐ Did I share my writing?

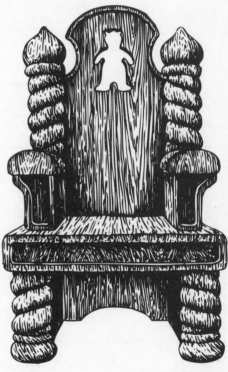

Now think about what you like about your writing. Use the space on the other side to tell about it.

Telling About My Writing

_____

I like my writing because _____

_____

_____

_____

_____

_____

_____

_____

_____

_____

_____

_____

_____

_____

_____

Words That Show Action

A verb is a word that shows action.
Look at the picture.
Finish each sentence with a verb from the box.

falls	hop	shines	runs	eat

1. The sun _____ brightly.

2. A leaf _____ softly.

3. The birds _____ quietly.

4. The puppy _____ quickly.

5. Five frogs _____ .

© Silver Burdett & Ginn

Look at the picture.
Write an action word to finish each sentence.

At the Circus

_____

- - - - - - - - - - -

1. The monkeys _____ .

_____

- - - - - - - - - - -

2. One clown _____ on the ground.

_____

- - - - - - - - - - -

3. A man _____ .

_____

- - - - - - - - - - -

4. The woman _____ on the rope.

_____

- - - - - - - - - - -

5. Some cubs _____ .

Adding s to Action Words

Look at Puff in each picture.
Write the action word from the box
that tells what the cat does.
Remember to add **s** to an action word for
one person or thing.

eat	read	run	jump	sleep

1.

_____

2.

_____

3.

_____

4.

_____

5.

_____

Name_____

Look at the picture.
Write action words to finish the story.

The Show

Some animals put on a show.

_____   _____

The dogs _____ . A bird _____ .

_____

The cow _____ . Then the dancers come

_____

on stage. Some worms _____ .

_____

A big rabbit _____ . Finally all the animals

_____

bow. Then the other animals _____ loudly.

Adding ed to Action Words

Write an action word from the box to
finish each sentence.
Remember to add **ed** to an action word
to tell about the past.

walk	pour	pick	add	wash

_____

1. Yesterday I _____
some berries.

_____

2. I _____ home with
a full basket.

_____

3. My dad _____ them.

_____

4. We _____ them in
a bowl.

_____

5. Last we _____ milk.

Write about what you did yesterday.
Use the action words in the box.

watched	helped	played

_____

6. At home I _____

_____

_____ .

_____

7. At school I _____

_____

_____ .

_____

8. Outside I _____

_____

_____ .

9. Write about something else you did yesterday.

_____

_____

_____ .

Unit 3, Lesson 8 • Use after page 78.

Adding s or ed to Action Words

Finish the sentences.
Add **s** or **ed** to each action word.
Remember that **s** tells about now.
Remember that **ed** tells about the past.

1. Last week the class _____ **pick** _____ a movie to see.

2. Yesterday the teacher _____ **show** _____ the movie.

3. Yesterday the class _____ **watch** _____ the movie.

4. Today the teacher _____ **ask** _____ questions.

5. Now the class _____ **talk** _____ about the movie.

Write about what your class did yesterday.
Write about what your class is doing today.
You may use action words from the box.
Remember to add **s** or **ed**.

| clean | play | learn | walk | paint | work | talk |

_____

- - - - - - - - - - - - - - -

6. Yesterday morning our class _____

_____

- -

_____ .

_____

- - - - - - - - - - - - - - -

7. Yesterday at recess our class _____

_____

- -

_____ .

_____

- - - - - - - - - - - - - - -

8. Today our class _____

_____

- -

_____ .

Unit 3, Lesson 9 • Use after page 79.

Opposites

Look at each picture.
Draw or find a picture that shows its opposite.
Then write the correct word.
Remember that words such as **fast** and **slow**
are opposites.

hot

1.

_____
- - - - - - - - - - - - - -
_____

little

2.

_____
- - - - - - - - - - - - - -
_____

day

3.

_____
- - - - - - - - - - - - - -
_____

Here are two buildings.
Write what is different about them.
Use opposites.

This building is _____ .

It is _____ the stairs.

It is on a _____ street.

This building is _____ .

It is _____ the stairs.

It is on a _____ street.

© SILVER BURDETT & GINN

Words That Tell Where

Read each set of directions.
Look at the pictures.
Circle all the words that tell **where.**

How to Make a Bow

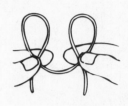

Make two loops.

Put one loop behind the other.

Push the front loop into the hole.

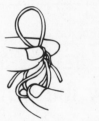

Bring it through the hole.

Pull tightly.

How to Sew a Button

Place the button on the shirt.

Put the needle under the shirt.

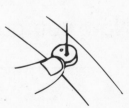

Push it into the button hole.

Then push it up.

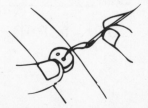

Pull the needle out the other side.

© Silver Burdett & Ginn

Look at the map.
Finish the directions.
Use words that tell **where**.

_____

‒ ‒ ‒ ‒ ‒ ‒ ‒ ‒ ‒ ‒

1. Walk _____ the field.
Follow the path.

_____

‒ ‒ ‒ ‒ ‒ ‒ ‒ ‒ ‒ ‒

2. You will be_____ two posts.
Turn left.

_____

‒ ‒ ‒ ‒ ‒ ‒ ‒ ‒ ‒ ‒

3. Now you are_____ the pond.

_____

‒ ‒ ‒ ‒ ‒ ‒ ‒ ‒ ‒ ‒

Go _____ the bridge.

4. Look for the big tree.

_____

‒ ‒ ‒ ‒ ‒ ‒ ‒ ‒ ‒ ‒

5. My house is _____ it.

Name_____

Researching

You just read a story about ways people travel.
Look at the family in these pictures.
Read the sentences that tell what they do
first and next.
On the back of this sheet, draw what you
think happens last.
Finish the sentence that tells about your picture.

First the family gets on a bus.

Next the family rides away.

Checking My Work ✔

◇ Did I begin each sentence with
   a capital letter? ☐

◇ Did I end each sentence with a period ⊡
   or a question mark ☐ ? ☐

◇ Did I put my sentences in story order? ☐

Last they _____.

© SILVER BURDETT & GINN

Name _____

Writing About
How We Go Places

Read each question. Check ☑ if you can answer yes.

☐ Did I write about how people go places?

☐ Are there any words I do not need?

☐ Did I draw a line through any words I did not need?

☐ Did I make a neat copy of my writing?

☐ Did I share my writing?

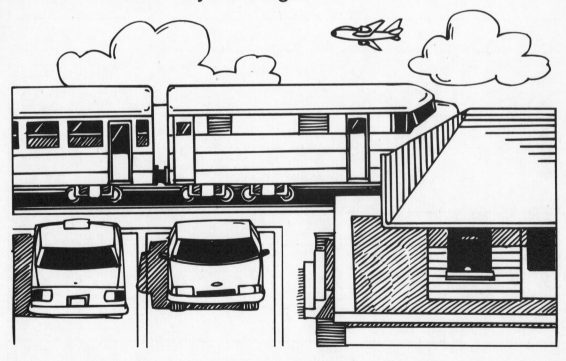

Now think about what you like about your writing. Use the space on the other side to tell about it.

Telling About My Writing

_____

_____

I like my writing because _____

_____

_____

_____

_____

_____

_____

_____

_____

_____

_____

_____

Words That Describe

The Prince is looking for Cinderella.
He writes a notice for the newspaper.
He hopes that Cinderella will read it.
Help the Prince finish his notice.
Write a describing word from the box
for each sentence.

glass	small	big	shiny	pretty

_____

1. Does this _____ shoe belong to you?

_____

2. It is a _____ slipper.

_____

3. I saw it on a _____ girl.

_____

4. She has _____ feet.

_____

5. She also has a _____ smile.

Little Bo Peep has lost her sheep.
She writes a notice for the newspaper.
Read the notice. Then make it better.
Add a describing word to each sentence.

Lost

Have you seen my sheep?
They are sheep.
Some have spots, too.
I miss my sheep!

Lost

_____
- - - - - - - - - - - - - - - - -
_____
- - - - - - - - - - - - - - - - -
_____

_____

_____
- - - - - - - - - - - - - - - - -
_____

Color Words

Ken drew this picture in his journal.
Use the color chart to color the picture.
Then write a color word to complete each sentence.

1 = red
2 = yellow
3 = blue
4 = green
5 = brown
6 = black
7 = purple
8 = orange

_____

- - - - - - - - - - - - - -

1. The _____ sun is bright.

_____

- - - - - - - - - - - - - -

2. The _____ house is new.

_____

- - - - - - - - - - - - - -

3. The boy wears a _____ shirt.

_____

- - - - - - - - - - - - - -

4. He has a _____ dog.

Now it is your turn.

Draw and color a picture.

Then write color words to label the things you drew.

Number Words

Pretend that you are visiting this farm.
You list all of the animals that you see.
You want to tell how many of each animal, too.
Look at the picture to find out how many.
Write the number words to complete the list.

_____   _____

1. _____ cows   2. _____ ducks

_____   _____

3. _____ hens   4. _____ horse

_____   _____

5. _____ eggs   6._____ goats

Now think about a trip to the circus.
Draw what you might see.
Count each thing you draw.
Make a list.
Use number words to tell how many.

Number Word	**Naming Word**
_____	_____
_____	_____
_____	_____
_____	_____
_____	_____
_____	_____
_____	_____

Words for Size and Shape

Read the poster.
Complete each sentence.
Use the words **large**, **small**, **round**, and **square** to tell about size and shape.

Come to Tyler's Toy Museum
We have toys in all sizes and shapes.

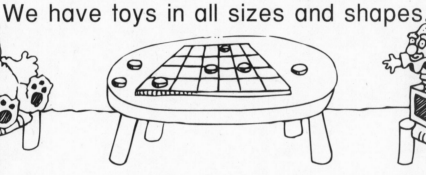

_____

1. Crawl into our _____ playhouse.

_____

2. A _____ bear waits inside.

_____

3. There is a _____ table to sit at.

_____

4. You can play checkers on a _____ board.

Draw a picture of your favorite toy.
Write a sentence to tell about it.
Use words that tell about size and shape.

Words That Compare

Who won the race?
Write the word **fast** in the sentences.
You may need to add **er** or **est**.

1. Jan is _____ .

2. Bill is _____ than Jan.

3. Kate is the _____ of all.

Pick two classmates and have a contest.
Jump to see how high you can jump.
Write each person's name.
Then write the word **high** in the sentences.
You may need to add **er** or **est**.

_____   _____

- - - - - - - - -   - - - - - - - - -

4. _____ jumped _____ .

_____   _____

- - - - - - - - -   - - - - - - - - -

5. _____ jumped _____ .

_____   _____

- - - - - - - - -   - - - - - - - - -

6. _____ jumped the _____ .

Name_____

Describing

You just read the story <u>Raccoons and Ripe Corn.</u>
Pretend that you are walking in this farmer's field.
What is growing there?
On the back of this sheet, finish the story.
Write about what you see.

Checking My Work ✔

◇ Did I begin each sentence with
a capital letter? ☐

◇ Did I end each sentence with a period ·
or a question mark ? ? ☐

◇ Did I put my sentences in story order? ☐

I am on the farm. I see _____

_____

- -

_____

_____

- -

_____

_____

- -

_____

_____

- -

_____

_____

- -

_____

_____

- -

_____

Name _____

Writing a Description

Read each question. Check ☑ if you can answer yes.

☐ Did I write a description of a windy day?
☐ Do I need to add any words?
☐ Do I need to cross anything out?
☐ Did I make a neat copy of my writing?
☐ Did I share my writing?

Now think about what you like about your writing. Use the space on the other side to tell about it.

Telling About My Writing

_____

- - - - - - - - - - - - - - - - - - - -

I like my writing because _____

_____

- - - - - - - - - - - - - - - - - - - -

_____

_____

- - - - - - - - - - - - - - - - - - - -

_____

_____

_____

- - - - - - - - - - - - - - - - - - - -

_____

_____

_____

- - - - - - - - - - - - - - - - - - - -

_____

_____

_____

- - - - - - - - - - - - - - - - - - - -

_____

Words for Sounds

Here are pages for a picture book
of neighborhood sounds.
Write **loud** or **soft** to tell about each sound.

1.

2.

3.

4.

5.

Make your own page for a picture book.
Draw a picture of something
you can hear.
Write **loud** or **soft** to tell about the sound.

Words for Touch

The words in the box describe how things feel.
Write a describing word for each picture.

cold	hot	soft	wet

1. _____ snow

2. _____ fur

3. _____ pet

4. _____ dog

© Silver Burdett & Ginn

Write a sentence about each picture.
Use one of the describing words from the box
in each sentence.

cold	hot	soft	wet

5. The children are _____ .

6. They feel _____ .

7. The blanket is _____ .

8. The soup tastes _____ .

Unit 5, Lesson 7 • Use after page 143.

© SILVER BURDETT & GINN

Words for Tastes and Smells

Finish this food poster.
Write a word from the box under each picture.
The word should tell how the food tastes or smells.

salty   sour   sweet   fresh

1. _____

2. _____

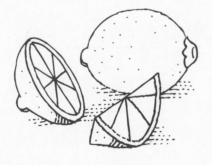

3. _____

4. _____

© SILVER BURDETT & GINN

Write a sentence that tells about each picture.
Your sentences should tell about how food
tastes or smells.
The words in the box will help you.

| salty | sour | sweet | fresh |

5.
_____
- -
_____

6.
_____
- -
_____

7.
_____
- -
_____

8.
_____
- -

Unit 5, Lesson 8 • Use after page 144.

Weather Words

Pretend that you are telling about
the weather on TV.
Use these pictures to help you.
Write a word from the box to describe each picture.
Remember that these words describe weather.

sunny	windy	cloudy	snowy	rainy

1. _____

2. _____

3. _____

4. _____

5. _____

Name _____

Now you can tell about something you
like to do outside.
Draw a picture.
Write a sentence about it.
Be sure to use a weather word.

On a _____ day, I like to

_____

_____

_____ .

© SILVER BURDETT & GINN

Words with Almost the Same Meaning

Here is Mia's story.
Read the pairs of sentences.
Circle the words that mean almost the same thing.

1. The story starts in a forest.

   The princess begins to cry.

2. Then a friendly troll comes.

   He arrives just in time.

3. Can you fix my bike?

   I hope you can repair the wheel.

4. The wheel hit that stone.

   That rock made a big hole in it.

5. The troll is happy to help the princess.

   Now the princess is glad too.

Read Ann's story.
Change each underlined word to a new word.
Make the new word mean almost the same thing.
The words in the box will help you.

beautiful **ocean** **jumped** **ship**

6. One day my family went to the blue <u>sea</u>.
   _____

   We liked our day at the _____.

7. Dad took us for a <u>boat</u> ride.
   _____

   The _____ sailed far from land.

8. Big fish <u>leaped</u> out of the water.
   _____

   They _____ and played all
   around us.

9. It was <u>pretty</u> to watch the sun set.
   It was
   _____

   a _____ day.

Unit 5, Lesson 10 • Use after page 146.

© SILVER BURDETT & GINN

Name

Persuading

Sometimes you may get a letter like the
one in The Jolly Postman.
Sometimes you may get a box.
What is in the box in the picture?
Write your story on the back of this page.

Checking My Work ✔

◇ Did I begin each sentence with
  a capital letter?   ☐

◇ Did I end each sentence with a period ⊡
  or a question mark ⍰ ?   ☐

◇ Did I use describing words?   ☐

Name

Name _____

Writing a Letter

Read each question. Check ☑ if you can answer yes.

- ☐ Did I write a letter?
- ☐ Did I ask someone to visit me?
- ☐ Did I write about something fun we could both do?
- ☐ Do I want to add any words?
- ☐ Do I want to cross anything out?
- ☐ Did I make a neat copy of my writing?
- ☐ Did I share my writing?

Now think about what you like about your writing. Use the space on the other side to tell about it.

Telling About My Writing

_____

I like my writing because _____

_____

_____

_____

_____

_____

_____

_____

_____

_____

_____

_____

Special Names

Finish each sign.
Remember that the names of people, pets, and places begin with capital letters.

1. Write the name of a person.

Hello!
My name is
_____
- - - - - - - - - - - - - - - -
_____

2. Write the name of a pet.

3. Write the name of a city or town.

Welcome to
_____
- - - - - - - - - - - - - - - -
_____

4. Write the name of a person.

This book belongs to:
_____
- - - - - - - - - - - -
_____

Rewrite the sentences.
Write the special names correctly.

5. mark and his horse rode to el paso.

_____

_____

_____

6. mia took her rabbit when she moved to ohio.

_____

_____

_____

Days of the Week

Read this story about Mark.
Write the correct day next to each thing on the list.
Remember that the days of the week begin
with capital letters.

   Mark takes piano lessons on Monday. He goes to
art class on Tuesday and Thursday. He plays
baseball on Wednesday and Friday.

Day of the Week	
_____	take piano lessons
_____	go to art class
_____	play baseball
_____	go to art class
_____	play baseball

What do you want to do after school?
Write the name of each school day.
Then write what you would like to do.
You can use the ideas below.

go to the park   bake   swim
paint   play ball   dance
fly a kite   visit Grandma ride a horse

Day of the Week	What I Want to Do

© SILVER BURDETT & GINN

Unit 6, Lesson 8 · Use after page 168.

Months of the Year

Read each riddle.
Write the name of the correct month on the lines.
Remember that the months of the year begin with capital letters.

In this month some people skate on ice.
The days are cold and snowy.
A special day is New Year's Day.

_____

- - - - - - - - - - - - - - - - - -

The month is _____ .

In this month leaves turn red, brown, and orange.
The days are cool and windy.
A special day is Thanksgiving Day.

_____

- - - - - - - - - - - - - - - - - -

The month is _____ .

Think of your two favorite months of the year.
Finish each riddle to tell about each month.
Write the name of the month on the last line.

_____

In this month _____ .

_____

The days are _____ .

_____

The month is _____ .

_____

In this month _____ .

_____

The days are _____ .

_____

The month is _____ .

Using he, she, and it

Complete the sentence about each picture.
Write **he**, **she**, or **it** in place of the underlined words.
Remember that **he**, **she**, and **it** can take the place
of nouns or naming words.

Mr. Smith opens
his book store.

_____

_____

_____ opens his book store.

The girl helps the kitten.

_____

_____

_____ helps the kitten.

The bus goes up Main Street.

_____

_____

_____ goes up Main Street.

Here are some pictures from a school newspaper.
Write a sentence about each picture.
Begin each sentence with **he**, **she**, or **it**.

Unit 6, Lesson 10 • Use after page 171.

Using we and they

Here are some posters from a circus.
Write **we** or **they** to finish each one.
Remember that **we** and **they** name people.

Smiley and I are clowns.

_____

_____ make you laugh.

Bob and Eli train lions.

_____

_____ will surprise you.

Luis and Sue ride horses.

_____

_____ will do tricks.

Roz and I walk on wires.

_____

_____ walk above you.

This first-grade class is having a parade.
Here are the posters the students made.
Write a sentence using **we** or **they** to finish
each poster.

Rose and Steven have three dogs.

_____

- -

Chen and I will ride bicycles.

_____

- -

Ted and I will play the drums.

_____

- -

_____

Using I and me

Carl asked Mrs. Tome some questions.
Complete the sentences.
Write a word or group of words from the box.
Always write **I** with a capital letter.
Always name yourself last.

I	**me**	**me and my dad**	**my dad and me**
	my dad and I	**I and my dad**	

What do you like to do, Mrs. Tome?
_____
- - - - - - - - - - - - - - - - - - - -
_____ like to fly airplanes.

Who gave you flying lessons?
                    _____
                    - - - - - - - - - - - - -
My dad gave _____ the lessons.

Does your father still fly with you?
            _____
            -
Yes, _____

fly together.

Now Carl has some questions for you.
Write a sentence to answer each question.
Use **I** or **me** in each sentence.

What did you learn in school yesterday?

_____

- -

_____

- -

_____

What did you and your friends do at recess?

_____

- -

_____

- -

_____

Why do you like to come to school?

_____

- -

_____

- -

_____

Story Starter

Name_____

Informing

You just read the story Whistle for Willie.
Peter wanted to whistle so that he could
call his pet.
Look at these pets.
What kind of pet would you like to have?
Write about what you would do with your pet.
Use the back of this sheet.

Checking My Work ✔

◇ Did I begin each sentence with
   a capital letter?   ☐

◇ Did I end each sentence with a period ⦁
   or a question mark ❓ ?   ☐

◇ Did I write a sentence that tells
   the main idea?   ☐

Name

Name _____

Writing About Something
I Can Do

Read each question. Check ☑ if you can
answer yes.

☐ Did I write about something I learned to do?
☐ Do I want to change a word?
☐ Did I make a neat copy of my writing?
☐ Did I share my writing?

Now think about what you like about your writing.
Use the space on the other side to tell about it.

Telling About My Writing

_____

- - - - - - - - - - - - - - -

I like my writing because _____

_____

- - - - - - - - - - - - - - -

_____

_____

- - - - - - - - - - - - - - -

_____

_____

- - - - - - - - - - - - - - -

_____

_____

- - - - - - - - - - - - - - -

_____

_____

- - - - - - - - - - - - - - -

_____

_____

- - - - - - - - - - - - - - -

_____

Using is and are

Can you find out what Jan is writing about?
Write **is** or **are** in each sentence to find out.
Then write the animal name Jan is telling about.
Remember to use **is** to tell about **one**.
Use **are** to tell about **more than one**.

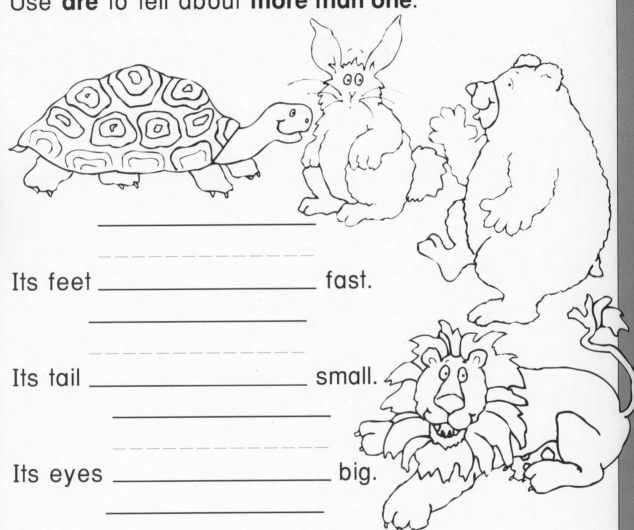

_____

Its feet _____ fast.

_____

Its tail _____ small.

_____

Its eyes _____ big.

_____

Its ears _____ tall.

_____   _____

It _____ a _____.

Write three puzzle sentences that tell about a thing.
See if your friends can guess what you wrote about.
Use **is** or **are** in your sentences.
You do not have to use words that rhyme.

_____

_____

_____

_____

_____

_____

_____

_____

_____

_____

_____

_____

Using <u>was</u> and <u>were</u>

Kim wrote about his trip to the seashore.
Write **was** or **were** in each sentence.
Remember to use **was** to tell about **one**.
Use **were** to tell about **more than one**.

_____

1. The sea _____ blue.

2. The birds _____ white.

3. The boat _____ fast.

4. My head _____ wet.

5. We _____ very happy.

Name_____

Write three sentences that tell about the picture.
Use **was** or **were** in each sentence.

6._____

_____

_____

_____

_____

7._____

_____

_____

_____

_____

8._____

_____

_____

Unit 7, Lesson 8 • Use after page 203.

Using have and had

Jill wrote about her new house in her journal.
Write **have** or **had** to finish Jill's work.
Remember that the word **have** tells about now.
The word **had** tells about the past.

_____

Last week we _____ an apartment.

_____

Now we _____ a big house.

_____

Last week I _____ a small room.

_____

Now I _____ my own room.

_____

Now I _____ a lot of new friends, too!

Pretend that Jill is a new classmate.
Tell her about your school.
Write three sentences about your school.
Use **have** or **had** in each sentence.

1._____

_____

_____

_____

2._____

_____

_____

_____

3._____

_____

_____

Using <u>go</u> and <u>went</u>

Timmy wrote a letter to his friend Alice.
Write **go** or **went** in each sentence.
Remember that the word **go** tells about now.
The word **went** tells about the past.

Dear Alice,

_____

Last week we _____ to the park.

_____

I _____ on a ride. Then my brother

_____

and I _____ into the pool. It was fun!

_____

Now we _____ on a school bus.

_____   _____

We _____ into the school. I _____

into Miss Fox's room. That is fun, too.

Your friend,

Timmy

Last week Timmy visited his friend Joe.
Today he and Joe go to a museum.
Write some more sentences for Timmy's letter.
Use **go** or **went** in each sentence.

_____

- - - - - - - - - - - - - - - - - - -

_____

- - - - - - - - - - - - - - - - - - -

_____

- - - - - - - - - - - - - - - - - - -

_____

- - - - - - - - - - - - - - - - - - -

_____

- - - - - - - - - - - - - - - - - - -

_____

Using see and saw

Read each of Maria's riddles.
Write **see** or **saw** in each sentence.
Remember that the word **see** tells about now.
The word **saw** tells about the past.

_____
- - - - - - - - - - -

1. Last year I _____ a kitten.

_____
- - - - - - - - - - -

Now I _____ a cat.

_____
- - - - - - - - - - -

2. Last week I _____ a seed.

_____
- - - - - - - - - - -

Now I _____ a plant.

_____
- - - - - - - - - - -

3. Yesterday I _____ clouds.

_____
- - - - - - - - - - -

Today I _____ rain.

Write your own riddles.
You can write about the pictures on this page.
Use the words **see** and **saw**.

_____ _____
- -

4. Last month I _____ an _____ .

_____ _____
- -

Now I _____ a _____ .

_____ _____
- -

5. Yesterday I _____ the _____ .

_____ _____
- -

Now I _____ the _____ .

_____ _____
- -

6. Last year I _____ a _____ .

_____ _____
- -

Now I _____ a _____ .

Name_____

Imagining

You just read a story about a rabbit who
hunts for spring.
The picture shows how different the weather can be.
It shows the weather in winter, spring, summer, and fall.
What time of year do you like best?
On the back of this sheet, write a story about your
favorite time of year.
Tell what you like to see and do.

Checking My Work ✔

◇ Did I begin each sentence with
a capital letter? ☐

◇ Did I end each sentence with a period ⊡
or a question mark ？ ? ☐

◇ Does my story have a beginning, a
middle, and an end? ☐

Name _____

Writing a Story

Read each question. Check ☑ if you can answer yes.

☐ Did I write a story?
☐ Did I tell how I lost and then found something?
☐ Do I want to change a word?
☐ Do I want to add any words?
☐ Did I make a neat copy of my writing?
☐ Did I share my writing?

Now think about what you like about your writing. Use the space on the other side to tell about it.

Telling About My Writing

_____

I like my writing because _____

_____

_____

_____

_____

_____

_____

_____

_____

_____

_____

_____

Parts of a Sentence

Tell about the picture.
Match the sentence parts.
Remember that a sentence has a **naming part**
and a **telling part**.
Then say each complete sentence.

1. Jodi   wears big shoes.

2. The children   has a birthday party.

3. The clown   has eight candles.

4. The cake   play games.

5. Jodi's dad   takes pictures.

© SILVER BURDETT & GINN

Jodi calls Grandma.
She tells her about the party.
What part is missing from each sentence?
Write a naming part or a telling part.

_____

6. My party _____

_____

_____ .

_____

7. _____

_____

_____ came to my party.

_____

_____

8. My favorite present _____

_____

_____ .

Word Order in Sentences

Help Fran write her book report.
Write the words in sentence order.

1. book This <u>Billy Bear</u>. is called

_____

- -

_____

_____

2. bicycle. a rides Billy Bear

_____

- -

_____

_____

3. funny is very book. It a

_____

- -

_____

_____

Write about a book you like.
Read each question.
Then write the answer in a sentence.
Remember to write words in sentence order.

4. What is the title of the book?

_____
- - - - - - - - - - - - - - - - - - -
_____
_____
- - - - - - - - - - - - - - - - - - -
_____

5. What happens in the book?

_____
- - - - - - - - - - - - - - - - - - -
_____
_____
- - - - - - - - - - - - - - - - - - -
_____

6. Why do you like the book?

_____
- - - - - - - - - - - - - - - - - - -
_____
_____
- - - - - - - - - - - - - - - - - - -
_____

Writing Telling Sentences

Your class is having a fair.
You want to put up a notice about the fair.
Read the information.
Then finish each telling sentence on the poster.

What: a fair
When: Friday afternoon
Where: the gym
Things to Do: eat, play games

Notice

_____

Our class is having _____.

_____

_____ on Friday afternoon.

_____

It is in _____.

_____

You can _____.

Now your class is putting on a play.
Read the information.
Then write a notice to send around the school.

What: a play
Time: 2 o'clock
When: Thursday
Where: the auditorium

Notice

_____

_____

_____

_____

_____

_____

_____

_____

_____

_____

Writing Asking Sentences

A new girl joined Maura's class.
Maura asked questions to find out about her.
Read each answer the girl gave.
Write the question Maura asked.

Q: _____

A: My name is Rosa Sanchez.

Q: _____

A: I live at 25 Oak Drive.

Q: _____

A: I moved here last week.

Q: _____

A: I have one brother and one sister.

Q: _____

A: I like my new school.

Pretend that a new student has joined your class.
Think of things you want to know about him or her.
Write five asking sentences.
Use the words in the box to help.

Who	What	When	Where	Why
How	Are	Do	Can	Will

My Writing Folder

Name _____

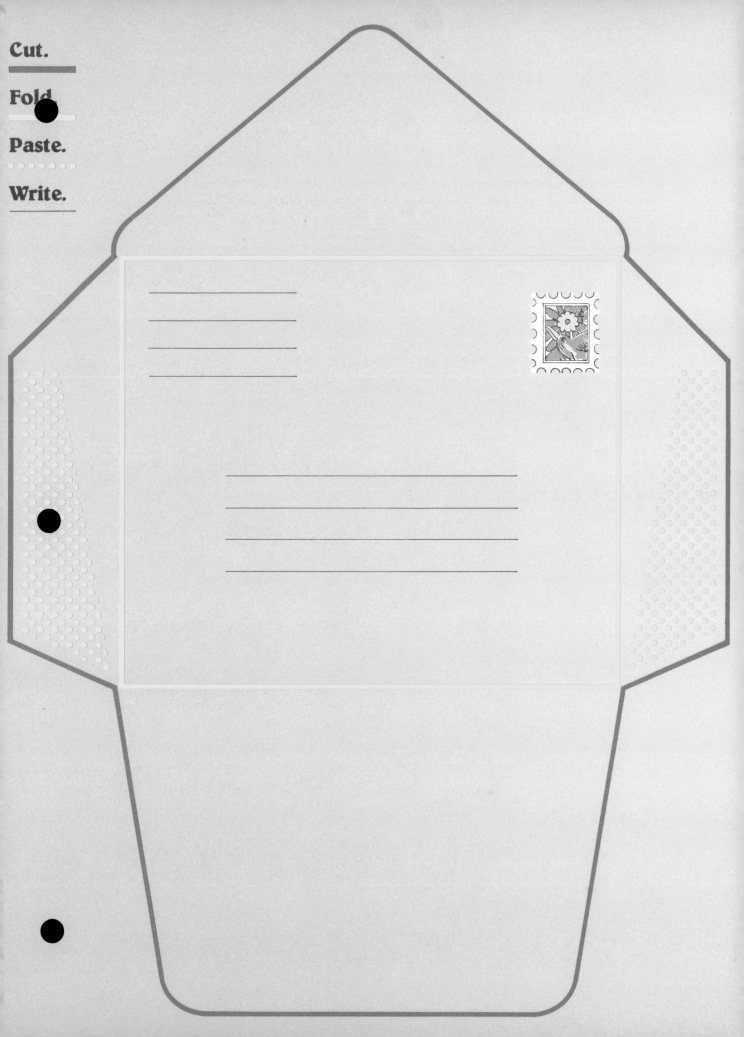

My Story

By

My Story

⬥

By _____